# *X-Con Xavier*

Book #24 of the Spirit of Truth Storybook Series

By Linda Mason

X-Con Xavier
Book #24 of the Spirit of Truth
Storybook Series

Author: Linda C. Mason

Self published by:
*Linda C. Mason*
*P. O. Box 1162*
*Powhatan, VA 23139*
LM.SpiritOfTruth@gmail.com
www.BooksByLMason.com

<u>Color Print</u>:

ISBN-13: 978-1-5356-0715-5

ISBN-10: 1-5356-0715-7

© 2014 by Linda C. Mason
Registration # TXu 1-925-200
Illustrated by Jessica Mulles
Edited by Nona Mason
All rights reserved

No part of this book, including contents and/or cover, may be reproduced in whole or in part (other than the activity pages) without the expressed written consent of the author.

Printed in the United States of America.

# X-Con Xavier

There was once a confused little boy,

Who never got to own a toy.

Angry and uptight

He cried ev'ry night

Violence and destruction he felt was a joy.

On and on this little boy went.

Thinking that's how his time should be spent.

When he came home

From the stores where he roamed

How to do what was right – he didn't have a hint.

His home life was full of fussing and fighting,

A drunken dad and strange cigarette lighting

No one really cared,

Quality time was impaired.

On his own as a child was very frightening.

He stayed in the streets most nights.

Very often ending up in street fights

He broke into cars,

Using stolen crow bars.

He thought he was soaring to great heights.

Of these empty works came no money,

No dreams, no goals -- not funny.

He pouted and he moaned

But now he's almost grown,

In a downward spiral alone, and unhappy.

At the half-way houses where he landed

Chaos and confusion, there he granted

Until one day

I'm sorry to say

He killed someone, and 30 years he was then handed.

X-Con Xa**v**ier was his nam**e**,

Violence **a**nd crime were his game.

Self-esteem a**n**d self-worth

Have been ba**d** since his birth

His life was a reflection of sha**m**e.

Fr**o**m the jail house to the State Penn he went,

Fast li**v**ing, drug using -- he was sp**e**nt.

His b**o**dy started to suffer

His mi**n**d couldn't recover

No way could he ever be confident.

One day he met a man named Rev. Tate.

The Good Book he would always take.

He stopped him between lunches,

To ask questions 'cause he had bunches

Tate answered, and didn't hesitate.

Why am I hat**e**d by the **C**reator?

The one who is called our Savio**r**

Is He r**e**ally up there?

Does He actu**a**lly care?

Or is He genuinely some kind of ha**t**er?

Was He watching when I was a boy?

Alone in my room with no toy.

Did He see me g**e**t licks?

During Dad's **d**runken fits,

Which dad sure did seem to enjoy.

Tate looked up and then he smiled

As he said, "si**t** here f**o**r awhile."

Con**s**enting t**o**, I did

Sit with him **a**s he slid

Out a pape**r that** unfolded for mil**e**s.

Written on these sheets in my hand

Are the steps to Salvation, God's Plan.

If you accept Him in your Heart

You will hear Him from the start.

Don't you want to feel like a whole man?

So Xavier took the pages from Tate.

It was early, only half past eight.

For up un**t**il right now

He had never known how,

So he took them and went t**o** medita**t**e.

As he studied about the life of Christ

How He was born and how He sacrificed

His heart began to feel

Compassion -- he began to heal

Oh how could God pay such a price?

Xavier began to profess

With his heart and his mouth he confessed

Even though he was hurt

Jesus' pain had been worse

He understood why his own life was a mess.

As he continued he learned to forgive.

He learned how better to live.

He shed all the pain

Got rid of the shame

And accepted the love God had to give.

Released finally and headed towards a new future

New hope, new heart, new picture

Once prison bound

Now heaven found

No more bitterness now filled his nature.

So when you think there's no hope

Another can throw you a rope

That can reach beyond places

That were once empty sp**a**ces

There's always one, who can he**l**p you cope**.**

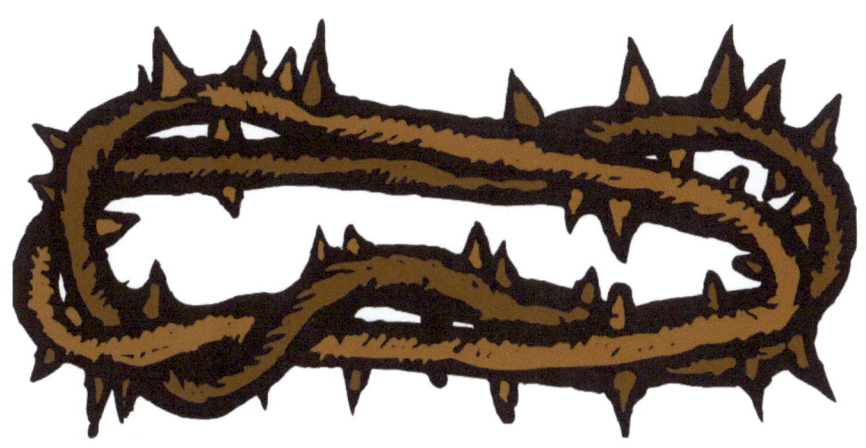

# Spirit of Truth Storybook
# Activity Page

1. *After reading the story, ask yourself the following questions:*

    - What did you like about the story?
    - What would you change about the story?
    - What could you have done to make things turn out differently?
    - Can you think of a way to help others after reading this story?

2. *Go back through the story pages and **decode your secret message**.*

    - Write the message on the lines below.
    - Send it to me through email at: www.BooksByLMason.com

I will send you back a personal comment. Be sure to include your gender and age.

# S.O.T. Messages of Encouragement Worksheet

(Fill in the missing letters on a <u>separate sheet of paper</u> or here, if you own the storybook, to unlock your *secret* message)

## *X-Con Xavier*

_ _   y _ _   h _ _   _   _ a _ _   _ _ _ _ .
L _ _ _ _   _ _   _ o _ g _ _ _   _ _ _
_ o _ _   _ _ .   _ _ _   w _ r _
_ r _ _ _ e _   _ _   s _ _ _ .   _ _ _ e
_ _ _   _ r _ _ _   _ _ _   c r _ _ _ _ _ _ .

**3. If there are puppets in your book,** *cut out the finger puppets and assemble as instructed. Be careful with your scissors.*

- Use your finger to help the character walk out a happy scene that you create

- When finished playing, place your puppet characters in a zip lock bag or an envelope, and store it between your favorite pages of the book, for safe keeping.

- Ask your parent or guardian if you can collect all 26 "Spirit of Truth Storybook Series" and remember to save the *Dove Cutouts* and glue them into the proper places on the chart.

### Dove Cut Out Letter

Receive **15% discount coupon** off of the purchase of my Editor's Edition of "**The Spirit of Truth**" Storybook Series, with proof of purchase from A - Z. This special edition will contain all 26 stories within one volume along with some added goodies. Fill out the chart below and **please print** all information clearly.

| A | B | C | D | E | F |
|---|---|---|---|---|---|
| **G** | **H** | **I** | **J** | **K** | **L** |
| **M** | **N** | **O** | **P** | **Q** | **R** |
| **S** | **T** | **U** | **V** | **W** | **X** |
| **Y** | **Z** | | | | |

Glue your "**Dove Letter**" cutouts in the corresponding boxes, on top of the proper letter. Fill 26 spaces from A- Z. Then cut this page out and mail it to:

**Linda Mason
P. O box 1162
Powhatan, VA 23139**

Name _____

Address _____

State _____ Zip _____ Email _____

Darkness and clouds have gathered around me
Lord, I need a Sunrise
Lord, I need a Sunrise
And still my faith is rooted in thee
Keep me in your arms, even when I'm in doubt
Lord, I need a Sunrise
Comfort in the Sunrise
This storm has been raging for many days now
Lord, I need a Sunrise
Lord, I need a Sunrise
I'm right at my breakthrough, show me how
Lord, I need a Sunrise
Breakthrough in the Sunrise
Bless this storm and the end result
Lord, I need a Sunrise
Lord, I need a Sunrise
Even if this storm is totally my fault
Lord, I need a sunrise
Forgiveness in the Sunrise
I know I haven't been the best child of Yours
Lord, I need a Sunrise
Lord, I need a Sunrise
But that's what Your grace and mercy is for
Lord, I need a Sunrise
Mercy in the Sunrise
Continue to draw me into You
Lord, I need a Sunrise
Lord, I need a Sunrise
And bless me with Your miracle breakthrough
Lord, I need a Sunrise
Blessings in the Sunrise
Take my life into Your hands
Lord, I need a Sunrise
Lord, I need a Sunrise
Lead me to the place You and I understand
Lord, I need a Sunrise
Understanding in the Sunrise

My desires in life are no longer important
Lord, I need a Sunrise
Lord, I need a Sunrise
Your will be done.  My will is in Your hands
Lord, I need a Sunrise
Your will is in the Sunrise
This storm will pass and sun will shine
Lord, I need a Sunrise
Lord, I need a Sunrise
And I know the other side is Your will, divine
Lord, I need a Sunrise
Light in the Sunrise
I take all of my struggles and give them to You
Lord, I need a Sunrise
Lord, I need a Sunrise
I will never lose faith in Your goodness true
Lord, I need a Sunrise
God is in the Sunrise

*By Tamara Mason*

# Instructions for Making Finger Puppets

1. Cut figures out. Follow the dotted line.
2. Cut strips out. Follow the dotted lines.
3. Fold over strip and tape into a ring.
4. Tape ring on the back of the figure that you cut out.

# Cut out the Finger Puppets

# X-Con Xavier Brain Game Visual Activity

Can you find the 7 items out of place on this picture? List them on the lines on the next page under Brain Game answer sheet.

# Brain Game's Activity Worksheet

*Brain Game*

1._____

2._____

3._____

4._____

5._____

6._____

7._____

# Master Brain Game Answer Keys

## X-Con Xavier

*Corn Dog*

*Guitar*

*Rocket*

*Duck*

*Lollipop*

*Fire Hydrant*

*Camera*

# X-Con Xavier Word Search
*Circle each of the following words:*

| | | |
|---|---|---|
| Xavier | Dad | Toy |
| Fighting | Crime | Jail |
| Savior | Shame | Lock up |
| Renewed heart | Pain | Forgiveness |
| Cigarettes | Hope | Jesus |
| Cross | Love | Meditate |

| m | o | f | c | f | o | r | g | i | v | e | n | e | s | s |
|---|---|---|---|---|---|---|---|---|---|---|---|---|---|---|
| e | w | t | t | n | j | e | l | o | v | v | p | o | i | t |
| d | x | v | t | m | k | n | r | n | m | o | k | j | e | h |
| i | d | g | h | o | p | e | k | l | m | l | l | m | n | t |
| t | o | y | h | e | k | w | b | p | o | b | y | r | h | f |
| a | g | w | s | u | s | e | j | b | m | n | u | p | e | w |
| t | c | q | g | d | f | d | a | d | b | z | t | o | l | f |
| e | r | f | b | f | h | h | k | l | k | p | h | p | o | d |
| r | x | t | r | n | q | e | m | i | r | c | u | u | c | e |
| a | a | j | o | m | a | a | c | i | y | i | u | l | k | t |
| t | v | l | i | a | j | r | a | f | a | y | k | l | u | w |
| e | i | u | v | h | o | t | g | i | v | n | i | o | p | w |
| z | g | b | a | s | x | w | p | u | y | e | e | e | q | g |
| i | n | g | s | c | z | v | x | o | m | y | w | s | v | q |
| n | i | k | r | e | n | e | w | e | d | h | e | a | r | t |
| g | t | h | a | c | e | u | s | u | n | k | m | r | y | o |
| b | h | t | e | b | s | b | h | e | a | r | t | x | y | u |
| h | g | w | v | m | o | x | a | v | i | e | r | h | s | a |
| y | i | e | s | h | k | n | m | y | g | e | d | s | o | v |
| t | f | y | s | e | t | t | e | r | a | g | i | c | h | d |

37

# X-Con Xavier Word Search
*Answer key*

| m | | | | f | o | r | g | i | v | e | n | e | s | s |
|---|---|---|---|---|---|---|---|---|---|---|---|---|---|---|
| e | | | | | | e | | | | v | | | | |
| d | | | | | | n | | | | o | | | | |
| i | | | h | o | p | e | | | | l | | | | |
| t | o | y | | | | w | | | | | | | | |
| a | | | s | u | s | e | j | | | | | | | |
| t | | | | | | d | a | d | | | | | l | |
| e | | | | | | h | | | | | | | o | |
| | | | r | | | e | m | i | r | c | | | c | |
| | | | o | | | a | c | | | | | | k | |
| | | l | i | a | j | r | | | | | | | u | |
| | | | v | | o | t | | | | n | i | a | p | |
| | g | | a | s | | | | | | | | | | |
| | n | | s | | | | | | | | | | | |
| | i | | r | e | n | e | w | e | d | h | e | a | r | t |
| | t | | | | | | s | | | | | | | |
| | h | | | | | | h | | | | | | | |
| | g | | | | | x | a | v | i | e | r | | | |
| | i | | | | | | m | | | | | | | |
| | f | | s | e | t | t | e | r | a | g | i | c | | |

*Spirit of Truth Storybook Series*

**APPROPRIATE AGE LEVEL
COLOR CODING KEY**

*The reading level for these stories is grade 5, but they can be understood and enjoyed by younger children, when read to them by older children or adults. The storybook covers have been colored to reflect the average comprehension levels for the following age groups.*

**Ages 4 and 5 = GREEN COVERS
Ages 6 and 7 = BLUE COVERS
Ages 8 and 9 = ORANGE COVERS
Ages 10 and above = RED COVERS**

*A special inspirational message has been coded throughout each story to help create 'added focus,' as well as, a visual tool for interactive concentration.* **Decode your secret message (written in red lettering throughout the story)** *and send it to me, along with your name and age, through my personal email address on my website at www.BooksByLMason.com and you will receive a personal email response from me. Some of the letters of the secret message have already been provided to assist you in your decoding. Additionally, <u>an added bonus</u> finger puppet activity, brain games, puzzles or other goodies, awaits each reader in the back of every storybook. An added "Treasure Hunt" can be found throughout the illustrations from my collection of storybooks, **<u>which details of this treasure hunt can only be found on my website.</u>***

*Also, E-Book Editions of this collection of storybooks, having no activities in the back of the books, as well as A Collector's Edition of this 26 Storybook Series is forthcoming. The collector's edition will include all 26 stories in the same book or 2 Volumes; at which time, the Master's List of every inspirational message will be revealed.*

1. *Anxious Arlene:* This story is about an *anxious* family consisting of a young brother and sister who lives with their grandpa and grandma. They have a little adopted dog that was never claimed or found by the original owner, and they all live together (with a few mishaps), in a loving, exciting home. This story can be enjoyed by children ages five and up.

2. *Busy Benny:* This story is about a busy little boy who loves to tinker with Wacky car models. He gets the opportunity to create a child sized Wacky car, with the help of his mom and dad, and finally enters it into a race with him doing the driving. He runs into a little surprise during his test run. This story can be enjoyed by children ages seven and up.

3. *Catty Carla:* This story is about a group of neighborhood house cats who carry on 'catty' conversations behind their friend's back at times. One particular Burmese cat soon realizes that her behavior was not appropriate, and it could be a little late for apologies. This story deals with death portrayed through animal characters. This book is dedicated to my daughter, Tamara, who as an adult, loss a cat she adored, Dr. Jeckyl, to an illness. The story line is very light; however, use parental wisdom. This story can be enjoyed by children ages five and up.

4. *Doubtful Denise:* This story is about a single father raising a young teenaged daughter who is full of doubt about herself, her abilities, and her future. Through a father's persistent encouragement and unyielding love for her, she eventually gains trust in herself and finds hope for a brighter future. This story can be enjoyed by children ages seven and up.

5. *Excited Ernesto:* This story is about a teenaged boy overcoming a fear of riding roller coasters. He experiences some exciting events at the county fair with a buddy friend of his and his buddy's sister, Maria. She adds extra excitement for Ernesto because no one knew she would be there, and he has a secret crush on her. Join this exciting group of youth as they sample the tasty treats found at all State Fairs, and as they experience some of the thrills of riding a roller coaster for the first time. Ride along with Ernesto, as your heart races to the beat of his own. This story can be enjoyed by children ages seven and up.

6. *Fearless Freddie:* Freddie is a little boy who is very creative and willing to test out any new adventure, regardless of risk. He is always ready and willing to try dangerous stunts until one day it gets him into big trouble. Does he learn from making dangerous choices, or does he continue to believe he is *invincible?* This story can be enjoyed by children ages five and up.

7. *Graceful Gregory*: Gregory loves to dance. He encounters teasing by his peers, but continues to do what he loves. He eventually meets another little boy who is not so interested in dancing, but his family is insisting that he gives it a try. The two boys meet and things begin to change for both of them. This story can be enjoyed by children ages seven and up, but younger if the reader is already dancing.

8. *Hopeful Henry:* Henry is full of anticipation for the new school year and is hopeful he will not experience the disappointments he has had in the past. He apparently gets disappointed over, and over again until a tragedy occurs in his life and he ends up being supported by the very people he thought were insignificant. He learns also, not only to see things differently, but to always be grateful and remain hopeful. This story can be enjoyed by children ages seven and up.

9. *Itchy Irvin:* This story is played out using a pack of dogs as characters. One of them misjudges some physical symptoms of another dog, and begins teasing him. That dog gets picked on constantly because of a skin condition. This particular *pack of dogs* meets a little boy who is going through a similar situation with his classmates at school. Let's see how this doggy story barks out. This story can be enjoyed by children ages seven and up.

10. *Jumping Josey:* This story is about a teenager who lives a life of thrills, while flipping and jumping, every chance she gets. She ultimately gets to experience one of her life's dreams -- sky diving. Travel with Josey as she goes on the most exhilarating jump of her life. This story can be enjoyed by children ages seven and up.

11. *Kissing Kirkland:* This story is about a very affectionate little boy who spends his days and nights kissing all kinds of creatures. Eventually, his normal kissing routine lands him into big trouble when he gets attacked by a momma duck. Let's follow our adorable *Kissing Kirkland* through an average day at home and see how he survives some of the repercussions having a personality like this, may present. This story can be enjoyed by children ages five and up.

12. *Lonely Lucilia:* This story is about two teenagers that are best friends. They are forced to separate, due to a family relocation, to a different country. The storyline starts out in a coastal town in Fife, Scotland, where Lucilia and Dillard have lived all of their lives. Take this lonesome journey with Lucilia, as she is forced to move from the only place she's ever known, and from her very best friend in the world, to a strange country she knows nothing about -- the United States of America. This story can be enjoyed by children ages eight and up.

13. *Muddy Maria:* This story explores the life of a little girl who loves to get dirty. With the help of her creative mother, her *dirty,* playful habit is channeled into a very productive fun activity. Dive in to this interesting twist of events and discover how playing in a lot of dirt, in some situations, can possibly turn out to be good for you. This story can be enjoyed by children ages five and up.

14. *Noisy Nelly:* This story explores the hatching of a bird from a bird's perspective. As this special bird explores her new world, words of wisdom flow from its mother. These words eventually take root in Nelly's heart in a very unique way. Soar with Nelly as she learns a very important lesson by refocusing her perspective on a part of her life she once perceived as gloomy. This story is dedicated to my first grandchild, Niyah Nylliana Mason, whom I believe one day will also soar as high as an eagle. This story can be enjoyed by children ages seven and up.

15. *Orphaned Ophelia:* Most of this story takes place in a very unique orphanage. Ophelia lives with the discomforts of not having a traditional family, but through it all she finds the compassion to help others. One day that compassion is returned, and she receives the most rewarding surprise of her life. This story can be enjoyed by children ages five and up.

**16. *Pudgy Pete*:** This story is about a little boy who obviously, because of his nickname, carries a little more weight than the average child. Journey with Pete as his self-pity and low self-esteem evolves into self-worth. After befriending a new *physically challenged* neighbor who moves in next door, she teaches him how to appreciate the special person he is, and not to focus on what size pants he wears. This story can be enjoyed by children ages seven and up.

**17. *Quarrelsome Quaniqua*:** This story contains **sensitive** material. It is not intended to be read as a *bedtime* story. Our story deals with a serious issue that some children must live with every day: **an abusive living environment** (non-sexual). The main character is a Latino teen (Quaniqua) who lives in poor, none-nurturing conditions. She becomes bitter and her behavior follows suit, until she meets someone outside of the home, and of a different culture, who finally treats her with respect. This causes Quaniqua to pull herself up and out of the pit she seemed to be falling into. Hang in there with her through the hard times, and see this young lady become a more productive, happier citizen. This story can be enjoyed by children eight and up; however, use parental wisdom as to if this story is suited for your particular younger child.

**18. *Reckless Ricardo*:** This story is about a young boy who starts out with some very reckless and disrespectful behaviors, but ends up with a very unusual science project that helps him start behaving in new, more respectful ways. You might be surprised at the results of this nontraditional outcome to a very common allergy. This story can be enjoyed by children ages seven and up.

**19. *Shy Stanley*:** This story is about a very quiet little boy who has some very interesting talents. He spends a lot of his time alone; however, he is extremely observant. Stanley meets a little girl with similar gifts and interests, which creates a bond that opens them both up to view their world differently. Let's visit these interesting young people and discover what their talents are. Maybe you have similar talents as well, and might have some interesting ideas of your own as to how to present those talents to the world. This story can be enjoyed by children ages seven and up.

**20.** *Tearful Tanya*: This story deals with a little girl who is full of grief over the passing of her grandmother. The family has a spiritual upbringing, and the little girl's mom guides her through the grieving process as she draws strength from above, where she's convinced her grandmother now resides. This story may be a little sensitive if you are a child in a similar situation, yet it can be enjoyed by children ages five and above.

**21.** *Ungrateful Ursula*: This story contains '**sensitive**' material. It is recommended for children ages ten and above. The story deals with a teenaged girl who grew up without her mother, and who very rarely saw her father. She lives temporarily with her aging grandmother. However, because of her grandmother's illness, Ursula must now live with her father, and she begins to use '*cutting*' as her method of coping. Things smooth out, but it's a very bumpy, painful ride. Walk with Ursula as she moves from '*much pain*' to '*much gain.*' This story can be enjoyed and read by children ages ten and above.

**22.** *Valiant Vivica*: This story is about a very gifted little girl who loves contact sports. Boys her same age seem to both admire her, and can be intimidated by her unprecedented strength at the same time. A natural disaster occurs on the day of Vivica's first wrestling tournament, and her valiant personality takes over. Follow along as she demonstrates extraordinary acts of bravery, and through it all, this experience will change her forever. This story can be enjoyed by children ages eight and above.

**23.** *Worrying Winston*: This story is about a little boy whose mother is an active Marine in the United States' Armed Forces. Winston is a very responsible little boy; however, he does worry a great deal about his mother's well-being. While on a *Treasure Hunt*, a game designed by his mother using riddles written in a letter Winston received, an unfortunate accident occurs and his mother ends up with a serious injury. Will they complete the Treasure Hunt*?* Stand with Winston and his father as they draw strength from each other to deal with a life's situation that changes their entire world. This story can be enjoyed by children ages eight and above.

**24. X-Con Xavier**: This story has been presented in '*limerick style poetry*' to lighten the seriousness of the topic for a child. Because of Xavier's destructive behavior, he is placed in various state institutions. Xavier meets a person while incarcerated that offers him hope and a different way of thinking. His inner spiritual change eventually points him in a new direction. Now with new hope, he has a chance to begin a new, more productive lifestyle outside of lock-up. This story can be enjoyed and read by children ages ten and above.

**25. *Yearning Yolanda***: This story takes you on a short journey with a twelve year old young girl who lost her eyesight in a car accident a year ago. She yearns for life to be as it was before the accident; however, life has a way of throwing you constant challenges that could cause you to either withdraw further into bitterness, or to emerge with a heart of gratefulness. Which one will Yolanda choose? Walk with Yolanda through an even harder challenge that, if handled with fear and bitterness, could not only take her life, but the lives of her mother and her best friend, Toby (her dog). This story can be enjoyed by children ages eight and above.

**26. *Zealous Zeporah***: Zeporah is a very passionate young lady full of enthusiasm for life. She jogged regularly, but one day she slipped and fell injuring her ankle. A situation such as this would have brought most people to a halt, or perhaps could cause others to go into a state of temporary depression. How will Zeporah handle a situation like this, when so many people are depending on her enthusiasm to help motivate them? This story can be enjoyed by children ages seven and above.

# About The Author

Minister Linda Mason is a unique ministry gift to the Body of Christ. Her experiences include the establishment of *Spirit of Praise Liturgical Outreach, Inc.*, a non-profit 501 © 3 organization, which not only helped to establish and oversee new dance ministries, but also extended into the communities.

In addition to the *Spirit of Truth Storybook Series*, Minister Linda has published *Appetizers from the Word of God... Are You Hungry?* Volumes 1, 2, & 3; which is an awesome tool for teaching foundational truths, in a simplistic manner, from God's Word.

Linda is a native of Suffolk, Virginia, the wife of George B. Mason, Jr., the mother of three; Tamara, Tiena, and George III. She has two adorable grandchildren, Niyah and Laana. Linda holds an Associate Degree in Early Childhood Education and has a passion for writing. She has written and is in the process of publishing these 26 children's stories from A to Z. Her plan is to have these unique stories available in both English and Spanish in the near future.

### What others have stated about this Series

- *Author Linda Mason's book, "Kissing Kirkland", is one of a series of books that tells a delightful story with a secret hidden valuable message for children. Her stories will captivate her audience with a variety of age appropriate activities to enhance each child's learning. As an educator for many years, I highly recommend her books!* **By Amelia Hopkins, a high school counselor.**

- *Linda Mason has done an excellent job using her creativity and insight in writing this series of books, the* **Spirit of Truth Storybook Series from A-Z**. *Each book deals with a subject or situation, such as a particular disability, or set-back that a child might encounter and have difficulty dealing with. The books offer resolutions that are positive and encouraging, helping a child build strength, confidence and maturity. The activities in the back of each book reinforce the lesson learned. The graphics are colorful and eye-catching, and each book's vocabulary is age appropriate. Each book is color coded to fit each age group, so there are appropriate books for every child's age. These are books your children will want to read or hear over and over; read by a big sister or brother. And they also have the opportunity to communicate with the author directly! I highly recommend these books for your children and grandchildren!* **By Nona J. Mason, a retired teacher, mother and grandmother.**

www.ingramcontent.com/pod-product-compliance
Lightning Source LLC
Chambersburg PA
CBHW040056100426
42734CB00034B/21